# In A Week

Di Kamp

Dr Kamp is founder and associate director of Meta UK Ltd. The company specializes in helping organizations and individuals to move towards excellence in the areas of leadership, culture and team performance.

Di has helped a number of organizations to enhance their performance development systems, and has trained both managers and their appraisees in how to use appraisals effectively to enhance performance.

She is also author of other business books including: *It's Not Rocket Science – A Blueprint for a Sustainably Successful Organisation* (Metabooks, 2015); *The 21st Century Manager* (Kogan Page, 1999); *and The Excellent Trainer* (Gower, 1996).

Teach<sup>®</sup> Yourself

# Appraisals In A Week

Di Kamp

First published in Great Britain in 1994 by Hodder Education.

This edition published in 2016 by John Murray Learning

Previous editions published 1998, 2012

*British Library Cataloguing in Publication Data:* a catalogue record for this title is available from the British Library.

ISBN 9781473608528
eISBN 9781444159783
1

Typeset by Cenveo® Publisher Services.

Printed and bound in Great Britain by CPI Group (UK) Ltd., Croydon, CR0 4YY.

John Murray Learning policy is to use papers that are natural, renewable and recyclable products and made from wood grown in sustainable forests. The logging and manufacturing processes are expected to conform to the environmental regulations of the country of origin.

Carmelite House
50 Victoria Embankment
London EC4 0DZ
www.hodder.co.uk

# Contents

**Introduction**    2

**Sunday**    4
Setting the context: why appraise?

**Monday**    18
Formulating an effective appraisal

**Tuesday**    34
The appraiser's role, I: setting the framework

**Wednesday**    50
The appraiser's role, II: attitudes and approaches

**Thursday**    66
The interview, I: reviewing achievement

**Friday**    82
The interview, II: looking ahead

**Saturday**    96
Completing the appraisal: after the interview

**7 × 7**    110

**Answers**    117

# Introduction

For over 40 years I have been working with organizations to enhance the way they appraise their staff. The main reason they need help is that appraisals are seen as an isolated and time-consuming round of paperwork which everyone has to engage in and few see any point to. My role is to help people to see how they can play a useful part in the development of the organization as a whole, and to make them a worthwhile and useful part of the staff development process. My intention in writing this book is to summarize the main themes that make a difference to the practice of appraisals.

It has become accepted practice in organizations to have a yearly round of appraisals. When we join a new place of work, we may be lucky enough to be trained in its appraisal system, which usually means being shown how to fill in the forms, or we may just learn how it's done by seeing how our line manager appraises us.

The consequence of this is that, for many of us, appraisals are just another set of paperwork to be completed, another time-consuming task to be fitted into our busy schedule. It's not a task we can rush through, either, as it requires us, as managers, to spend time with each person on our staff, working through the form and agreeing it with them.

Yet, if we were to truly recognize the potential and intended value of appraisals, they would be regarded completely differently.

The original intention of an appraisal system is to encourage and develop the staff of the organization, so that they all perform to their highest potential. Properly implemented and used, appraisals will help you, if you are a manager, to ensure that your staff are as effective as possible in their work, and thereby to make your area of work a powerful contributing factor to the success of the organization.

Appraisals can also make your job as a manager easier, because they give you the opportunity and framework to encourage and develop your staff. This results in a team of people who feel valued and supported, and who know that their work makes a positive difference to the organization as a whole. As a manager, you can then spend less time and energy on pushing and controlling your team, and more time on the work that moves things forward and is more satisfying.

In this book, we will look at how you can use appraisals to enhance the way your organization works and how they can encourage your staff to continually develop. It will give you guidance on what is important about appraisals and how they fit into the bigger picture of continuous improvement of performance. By the end of the final chapter, we hope that you will see how appraisals can make a positive difference to you as a manager, your staff as individuals, and the organization as a whole.

SUNDAY

# Setting the context: why appraise?

In this chapter, we will explore why it is important to set appraisals within the bigger context of the development of the whole organization, and consider the purpose and principles of appraisals. If appraisals are treated as an isolated piece of paperwork that comes round once a year and is stored in the filing cabinet until next year, or is sent to the HR department and never referred to again, then it becomes a waste of time and energy.

If, on the other hand, appraisals are seen as an important part of the overall success of the organization, then they take on a different meaning and become a vital part of everyone's role. If you are a director of the organization, you will want to ensure that everyone is working towards the same goals, and appraisals can help with this. If you are a manager of a team, you will want your part of the organization to be recognized for contributing to the whole and your team to give of their best, and appraisals can help. And as a team member, you will want to be valued for your work, and appraisals will provide a summary of that. Let's explore the importance of appraisals in the bigger context.

SUNDAY

MONDAY

TUESDAY

WEDNESDAY

THURSDAY

FRIDAY

SATURDAY

# The context

If we don't know what can be gained from effective appraisal then we have no reason to view it as a positive and useful activity.

Often it turns into a yearly 'chat' with the individual where neither side is sure what will come out of it.

As manager, you know that you're supposed to sound positive, no matter what. Yet most of those we will be appraising are neither 'stars' nor awful at what they do. What can you say when someone just does their job well? And what do you say when someone is not doing well and you are supposed to sound positive?

It is hard to give direction to the appraisal without a clear purpose, and the manager can feel solely responsible for trying to 'make it work'.

The individual being appraised, on the other hand, may fear that if they say the 'wrong thing', they will ruin any chances of promotion.

If you are using 360° feedback, they may also fear the effect of negative responses from others and wonder how to offset that effect.

It is important to be clear about how appraisals can contribute to organizational effectiveness, so that both sides use the opportunity well.

To achieve this clarity, we need to look at the purpose of having an appraisal system, and identify how it can benefit those involved.

# The purpose of appraisal

Appraisal means many different things in different contexts. Usually, in a work context, it implies some type of formal, recorded interview with every member of staff at regular intervals, e.g. yearly, and often seems to be isolated from the rest of the everyday contact between managers and their staff.

For us to use appraisal effectively, we need to see it as part of overall performance management and development.

We all like to know how we're doing as individuals, and organizations need to know how they match up to their goals and targets.

Often this is monitored in an informal way. After all, we're all very good at noticing if something isn't going according to plan, or isn't as good as we want it to be.

However, this informal monitoring tends to ignore the genuine progress and achievement that takes place.

We tend to assume that if no one says anything is wrong, then we're probably doing reasonably well! In organizational terms, this can be translated into: if we're still making a profit, we're doing OK.

Appraisal is designed as a means of monitoring the progress and achievement of the organization, to encourage and support the continuing development of that organization in a changing world.

This not only helps the organization as a whole to continue to work towards optimum effectiveness, but also provides departments and individuals within that organization with a clear overall development plan, into which their own development plans can fit.

For example, it will make far more sense to me that I should learn to use a computerized database if it is introduced into the organization with clear explanations of how it will contribute to the increased effectiveness of the organization.

If it seems that the database has been introduced just because there was some money spare in the annual budget, I am more likely to defend the old system, and resent the time I have to spend on the change.

Appraisal is also designed to encourage and motivate employees continually to develop their skills, so that they are of ever-increasing value to their organization. We will increase this motivation if we offer positive recognition of progress and achievement, as well as support and help in developing in those areas that are seen to be weaker.

Appraisals present the opportunity to give this recognition, and to identify with someone how they could improve in areas where they are weaker.

So both the individual and the organization gain from the process.

**Checklist: the purposes of appraisal**

- *To monitor the progress and achievement of the organization as a whole*
- *To encourage and support the continuing development of that organization in a changing world*
- *To encourage and motivate employees continually to develop their skills, so that they are of ever-increasing value to their organization*

# The benefits of effective appraisal

To ensure that appraisal is used well, rather than just paid lip service to, it is important that the benefits to all those involved are recognized and spelt out.

We all need to feel that the process will have a pay off for us personally. Then we will be prepared to invest some time and energy in it.

We also need to feel that it has some relevance, both short term and long term, to our professional and business development.

When we put into practice the principles and processes of appraisal effectively, then there is positive benefit and development for the appraiser, for the individual being appraised and for the organization.

It becomes a welcome and useful part of the employee's working life. It is also a vital part of the manager's role, both in offering support to his/her staff, and in maintaining the development of the organization. As managers, we need to be aware of the benefits and be able to state them to others, to make sure that appraisal is treated as something which has a valuable contribution to make to working life.

## Benefits for the organization

Organizations as a whole will gain from effective appraisals:

● by having motivated employees
● by learning what skills are available which can be drawn on to enhance their overall performance
● by being able to identify, before a problem arises, how they may need to train or develop their employees to meet organizational goals
● by having their finger on the pulse of the internal set-up.

## Benefits for the individual

What of the person being appraised? For the individual, appraisal provides an opportunity to:

● receive recognition and support from management as they develop in the work role

- be reminded of how they are contributing to the effectiveness of the organization overall
- voice their views and offer constructive suggestions on both their own development and that of the overall organization.

## Benefits for the manager

For the manager, the appraisal is an opportunity to:

- enhance the relationship with the individual
- give the individual recognition and support in their continuing development
- enhance the individual's motivation by reminding them of the overall context of organizational goals to which they are contributing
- evaluate the effectiveness of individual contributions to the overall effectiveness of the organization
- gather information which may help to develop further ways of enhancing organizational effectiveness.

## Principles of appraisal

So how do we turn the appraisal into this positive and useful tool?

Whether we are appraising on an informal or formal basis, there are guidelines to the approach to take which will make it far more likely that the appraisal has the effect we want.

The principles of appraisal provide a framework to define the approach, so that we undertake the appraisal with a clear idea of our intentions and purpose.

The overriding principle of appraising is that we encourage the person being appraised to take on more and more responsibility for his/her own development. In doing this, we need to remember that the individual will have some feeling of not being in control, at least initially.

Most times, an appraisal is imposed on us; but even if we have actively asked for it, we tend to do so because we don't feel that we can sort out any problems or a schedule for development ourselves.

We also need to remember that the individual knows more about their own achievement, progress and problems than anyone else – they experience it, as opposed to observing it!

So our intention in appraisal is to enable the individual to take more and more of an active part in identifying their own strengths and weaknesses, and in deciding what to do about them.

## An appraisal is an interaction between two people

In other words, the appraisee is human too, so we need to ensure that we treat them with respect, in order to build up trust.

If they do not feel that they can trust the manager, then the contribution they make will be limited, and the usefulness of the appraisal reduced.

If we do not come across as 'human', and accepting of them, then they will be intimidated. If they feel that we may use what they say against them in some way, then they will say as little as possible about any difficulties and problems they may have. As we all know, these will then show up at the most inopportune time, and cause us bigger problems because they affect the appraisee's work.

## Appraisals should have a positive intention and outcome

This requires that we set a positive tone to the whole appraisal. Positive recognition is important to all of us. We like it when someone says thank you, or remarks on something we've achieved or progressed in. We can offer this recognition in the appraisal, and thereby encourage the individual.

We also know that building on strengths is easier than putting the emphasis on correcting weaknesses.

Finally, we want to ensure that any weak areas are dealt with, so we need to offer constructive help to the individual in finding a way to improve performance. After all, being told that we were not doing well enough at something never helped us to do it better – it only made us feel worse.

**TIP**

**Checklist: the principles of appraisal**

- *The individual will take more and more responsibility for their own development and we will help them to do that.*
- *We will establish trust and a good relationship as the basis for the appraisal.*
- *An appraisal has a positive intention and outcome, and we will use it to help the individual to use their strengths well and identify ways of improving their performance.*

# The role of the manager in appraisals

Having looked at the purpose and benefits of appraisals, we can begin to identify the first stages of how we can ensure that appraisals are useful and constructive.

It is up to us, as managers, to set the context for the appraisal and educate our staff into viewing it as useful. We also need to remind ourselves of the potential of appraisal, so that we treat it as an important part of our responsibilities and prepare for it properly.

We are responsible for setting the tone which will help our staff to treat appraisal as a useful and constructive part of their overall development. This is especially important when appraisal has not been seen in this light before.

By thinking through our own way of expressing the benefits, purpose and intention of appraisal, we will already have begun the journey towards more successful appraisal.

# Summary

Appraisals are not worthwhile for the organization unless we set them in the bigger context of developing performance throughout the organization, in order to achieve organizational goals. Your staff will commit to their part in the appraisal process if they can see how it will benefit them.

To do this, we need to:

● Make sure the appraisal is seen as purposeful. This means that it is related to both the overall goals of the organization and to the contribution of the individual.

● Establish how the appraisal benefits the individual being appraised, their manager who appraises them, and the organization as a whole.

● Put the appraisal in the context of overall performance development, as a formal point of recognition of progress and achievement, and a plan for the next stage of development.

● Make it easy for the person being appraised to play their part in making it an effective, positive and useful appraisal. This includes ensuring that they understand its purpose and how it will benefit them.

● Remind ourselves of why appraisals are worth giving our time to, as managers, and what the principles are that we need to apply.

The following multiple-choice questions are a reminder of what we've covered today.

SUNDAY

MONDAY

TUESDAY

WEDNESDAY

THURSDAY

FRIDAY

SATURDAY

# Questions (answers at the back)

1. What is the purpose of appraisals for those being appraised?
   a) To have a yearly chat with an employee ❏
   b) To tell employees what they've not done well ❏
   c) To provide data to HR ❏
   d) To encourage and motivate employees to continually develop their skills ❏

2. What is the purpose of appraisals for the organization?
   a) To monitor the progress and achievement of the organization as a whole ❏
   b) To keep records on employees ❏
   c) To weed out those who aren't being effective ❏
   d) To decide on who gets a bonus ❏

3. How do effective appraisals benefit organizations?
   a) They have up-to-date records. ❏
   b) They motivate employees. ❏
   c) Their managers are kept busy. ❏
   d) They look good to shareholders. ❏

4. How do effective appraisals benefit individuals?
   a) They receive recognition and support from their manager. ❏
   b) They get a bonus. ❏
   c) HR are pleased with them for doing it. ❏
   d) They can tick something off their list of objectives. ❏

5. How do effective appraisals benefit managers?
   a) They can tick something off their list of objectives. ❏
   b) They can get rid of employees they don't see as effective. ❏
   c) HR stop bothering them. ❏
   d) They have enhanced relationships with their employees. ❏

6. What is the main principle of appraisals?
   a) To tell people what is wrong with their performance ❏
   b) To set the next year's objectives ❏
   c) To encourage employees to take responsibility for their own development ❏
   d) To say something nice to each person ❏

7. What should be the manager's intention when conducting appraisals?
   a) To get them done as quickly as possible ❏
   b) To drive home how important the objectives for the person are ❏
   c) To find something positive to say ❏
   d) To encourage the person to take an active part ❏

8. What tone should the manager set for the appraisals?
   a) Positive and constructive . ❏
   b) Friendly and informal ❏
   c) Structured and formal ❏
   d) 'Let's just get through this.' ❏

9. How should the manager want the person being appraised to approach the interview?
a) As being something to dread ☐
b) Ready to contribute ☐
c) Hoping they will be seen as OK ☐
d) Hoping it won't take long ☐

10. How should the manager approach the appraisal process?
a) As something to get done ☐
b) Ready to tell the person what they think of them ☐
c) As an important part of their job ☐
d) Wondering what they should say ☐

# MONDAY

# Formulating an effective appraisal

For an appraisal to be effective, it needs a clear framework to give it meaning, for both the manager and the employee. In this chapter, we will look at how you ensure that the appraisal is relevant to both parties, and is meaningful. It needs to relate to the organizational goals, the departmental objectives and the actual work the individual is expected to do. We will also remind ourselves that doing the job (i.e. the tasks) and doing the job *well* are different, and that we need to ensure that the appraisal references *how* the tasks are done, not just *if* they are or not.

To make an appraisal really effective, it needs also to give recognition to the individual person, so we will look at how you can bring in their personal qualities and their progress in developing personal and interpersonal skills. Finally, the appraisal needs to look to the future and be seen as developmental, indicating the areas where the person can grow further, so that they play their part in the continuous development of the organization. We will look at how that development can be identified and fed into the appraisal framework.

# Framework for appraisal

If we are going to conduct effective appraisals, we need to ensure that both sides are clear about what exactly is being appraised.

Of course we all know that we appraise performance, but we so often don't know exactly what that means in practice.

So we pick up on what we have noticed. This tends to be either outstanding performance or poor performance in a particular area or activity which happened recently.

This simply leaves our employee confused about what's important: 'Was my obvious lack of interest at the last staff meeting more important than consistently meeting my sales targets?'

Alternatively, if there is nothing we have noticed, we tend to make vague and general statements which closely resemble old-style school reports: 'Your work is generally fairly good, and you continue to make progress.'

Our employee is left with no clear picture of what we mean – probably because we don't know what we mean!

Even worse, we may then go on to ask them what they think. How can they comment when they don't know what we are looking at in their performance?

We need to make explicit, for ourselves and for those we appraise, what areas of performance are being considered.

# Formulating relevant appraisals

The first step in establishing what to appraise with an individual is to check what the organization as a whole is aiming towards.

Your organization's mission statement, or the company's aims and objectives will tell you this.

We need to frame what we are appraising in the larger context of what the organization has as its goals, so that it is seen as relevant, both for the organization and for the employee.

For example, suppose your company has, as part of its mission statement, 'putting customers first'. It will be important to look at how your staff deal with customers as part of their appraisal.

You may also have specific departmental goals, which are derived from the overall goals of the organization. For example, suppose your department has as one of its goals 'reduction of customer complaints'. It will be important to look at how your staff contribute to reducing customer complaints.

Answering the following questions will give us the first part of a framework for appraisal.

1 What is your organization's mission statement?
2 What areas of skill, behaviour or attitude does it imply for employees?
3 What are your department's goals?
4 What areas of skill, behaviour or attitude do they imply for employees?

These areas of performance will be relevant to your organization, because the appraisal will show how the individual is contributing to the organizational goals.

They will also make sense to the individual, by relating their individual achievements to what the organization as a whole wishes to achieve.

# Formulating a meaningful appraisal

The next step in establishing what to appraise with an individual is to ensure that what is appraised relates to their job specification.

If my duties and responsibilities include the management of an administrative records system, but my manager never refers to that in my appraisal, I may begin to wonder if the appraisal has anything to do with my real job – or whether that was an important responsibility after all!

Look at your employee's original job description and specification. (If this does not exist, ask them to help you to compile a list of main duties, responsibilities and requirements.) Then answer the questions below:

5 What are the main areas of performance to be appraised, based on the job description and specification?
6 What skills, behaviours or attitudes are required to fulfil this job specification?

We now have the basis for a relevant and meaningful framework for appraisal. Your answers to questions 2, 4, 5 and 6 above will identify for you the main criteria of a competent performance in this role.

You can use information from an appraisal based on these criteria to demonstrate how that person contributes to organizational and departmental goals.

The criteria are relevant and meaningful to the person being appraised because they can be shown to be related directly to the organization's goals and to their own job specification.

# A comprehensive appraisal framework

So far, we have looked at how to link the appraisal criteria to both the organizational goals and the individual's role. This ensures that the appraisal will have some relevance and meaning by making its links to the work context explicit. However, it is still easy to miss information or omit acknowledgement of an individual's progress or achievement.

More and more organizations are now acknowledging the importance of the individual's continuing personal and professional development. We live in a world where change has become the norm. We need individuals who show initiative, who are willing to learn, who are flexible.

It is therefore important that we have, within the appraisal framework, some means of identifying personal and professional achievements which are not strictly related to the narrow work context. They may, however, be evidence of an individual's developmental capacity.

For example, do you know if any of your staff:

● work as a volunteer in their community?
● run a scout group?
● are on the PTA for a local school?
● are taking an Open College course or evening class?
● are expert at climbing or orienteering?
● have recently learnt to sail, or speak a foreign language, or do karate?

These and many other out-of-work activities demonstrate that the person has talents and abilities which could well be transferred to the work context in some way.

They also demonstrate willingness to learn and to be involved – vital requisites in a changing organization.

Most organizations have some form of training and development programme for their staff. However, as managers, we do not always pick up on what courses or seminars our staff have attended, and what they may have gained as a result.

This is particularly true of training in so-called 'soft skills', those areas which are not directly related to specific knowledge or technical skill development.

The appraisal framework needs to pick up on any professional development that the appraisee has undertaken.

Finally, there is an area of performance appraisal which is often missed because it is hard to define. This is 'what we are like as a person to work with'. Remember the stereotype of the doctor's receptionist as a 'dragon'? And the 'ordinary' person in the office who always makes everyone feel comfortable and is liked by everyone?

There are people in organizations who fulfil their job specifications exactly, yet are uncooperative or even hostile with others. And there are those who do nothing extraordinary in their actual work role, yet help to create and maintain an excellent team atmosphere.

It is important that we notice and value how people are with others, and how that contributes to the effectiveness of the organization.

Using feedback from peers, subordinates and customers can significantly add to our awareness of how someone works with others. Encouraging the appraisee to ask others for their opinion of their behaviour and attitudes in relation to questions 2, 4 and 6 will add to the information about personal qualities. The answers to the following questions will also be helpful:

7 What activities or courses are your staff involved in, outside work?
8 What training or development have your staff undertaken, and how did it affect them?
9 What are the personal qualities required of your staff?

## Looking for development

In business these days, continuous improvement is a vital theme, both organizationally and individually. An appraisal system is intended to encourage the development of the individual.

We must ensure that the appraisal framework identifies and recognizes the employee's development. After all, if I have been doing this job for years I may be competent at it, yet make no effort to take it any further.

To some extent, the questions already identified will pull this out. To ensure that we have really identified development, we need some 'markers'.

At each appraisal we need to know how the person was performing at their last appraisal (or, if it's an initial appraisal, what their starting point is).

Then we need to assess with them how they have improved on that performance.

Finally, we need to agree with them how they will continue to improve their performance.

What often happens is that we only pick up on a need to improve where performance is poor. For example, if someone is lax with their record keeping, we ask them to 'get better at it'. If their work is already competent, we tend to just make lame statements like, 'Well done, keep up the good work.' This tends to bring two unwanted results:

- The individual's work standard actually deteriorates as they 'sit back on their laurels'.
- They are less motivated because there is nothing in particular to aim for.

The alternative is to ask them to identify how they could improve their performance even more, and encourage them to continue to develop their skills to do so. You need to answer the following questions:

10 How are your staff demonstrating continuous development?
11 What areas could you look at with them for further development?
12 What support and help is available to make these developments?

# Using the framework for appraisal

We can use this framework in two different ways, depending on what already exists as an appraisal system.

If you haven't already developed a formal written procedure for appraising, you can use the questions asked throughout this chapter to construct an appraisal format and recording framework.

The example below shows how these questions could be used as the basis for guiding both the appraiser and the appraisee in what to look for in an appraisal, and what to 'collect' as evidence.

**Example**

1 This company's mission statement implies that employees should demonstrate flexibility, a high standard of customer service and a willingness to develop their skills.

How have you (has this employee) demonstrated this?
2 This department's goals are to reduce customer complaints and to increase the speed of delivery of service.

How have you (has this employee) contributed to these goals?
3 Your main duties are: reception of visitors, answering telephone queries, processing of repairs procedures, maintaining the records of customer usage.

What are your (are your employee's) examples of best practice in this, and what exactly did you do?

What do you feel you (they) could improve on in your job performance, and how could you achieve that?

4 What are you (is your employee) involved in outside work which you feel demonstrates skills/abilities/potential which are important to you and/or your organization?

5 What training and/or development activities have you (has your employee) undertaken?

How have they been useful to you, personally or professionally?

6 What personal qualities do you have (has your employee got) which you feel contribute to your (employee's) value in this organization?

Give an example (examples) of how they have been used.

7 How are you (is your employee) developing your own work performance?

8 How else would you like to develop your work performance?

Notice how this set of questions makes clear what the areas for appraisal are. It ensures that all parties to the appraisal are working to the same criteria, and that those criteria are relevant to the organization and the individuals.

You can also use this framework to help those involved in appraisal to make the process meaningful.

You may already have a recording system for appraisal which asks general questions, or has general headings.

### Example

● Achievements over the last year
● Targets met
● Areas for improvement
● Agreed new targets

It may then be useful to use the questions above to help both parties prepare for the appraisal by using them as guidelines for what to discuss, in order to identify what to record in the different sections.

# Summary

In this chapter, we have looked at the different elements of an effective appraisal framework. This will enable both you and the employee to appraise the achievement, progress and potential of that person to play their part fully in the organization. By linking the framework to organizational objectives, departmental objectives, the individual's role and the qualities of that individual, you create something that is really meaningful.

There is work required to create a really careful and meaningful appraisal framework. It takes a while to clarify the links between an individual's job and the organizational and departmental objectives, and to clarify what really matters about how they do their work. However, this is a one-off task, and thereafter only requires occasional adjustment as the organization and the role develop.

The rewards for doing this preparatory work are that both you and the employee have clear criteria and expectations about their role, and can have genuinely useful conversations about what they do well and how they can develop further. By investing time in producing an appraisal framework, you will be making the rest of your preparation much easier, and will be able to conduct worthwhile appraisal interviews.

The following multiple-choice questions are a reminder of what we've covered today.

SUNDAY
MONDAY
TUESDAY
WEDNESDAY
THURSDAY
FRIDAY
SATURDAY

# Questions (answers at the back)

1. What do we appraise in someone's performance?
   a) How they are progressing against objectives ❏
   b) What we remember of their performance ❏
   c) What they have failed to do ❏
   d) Anything we can think of ❏

2. How do we link appraisals to the overall organizational development?
   a) We don't. ❏
   b) We link objectives to organizational goals. ❏
   c) We just use the functions people do. ❏
   d) We give a bonus if the organization is doing well. ❏

3. How does the appraisal reflect the person's job?
   a) Of course it is about their job. ❏
   b) By talking about how they do their job ❏
   c) By relating objectives to what their job requires of them ❏
   d) We hope they tell us what they have been doing. ❏

4. Why should we include personal qualities in the appraisal framework?
   a) We don't need to – it's not on the form. ❏
   b) They are important in how the person goes about their tasks. ❏
   c) It might make someone feel better if we tell them they are a nice person. ❏
   d) To have something to talk about ❏

5. Why is it useful to find out about a person's activities outside work?
   a) It's a nice thing to do. ❏
   b) It fills up the time. ❏
   c) They matter to them. ❏
   d) They may indicate possible areas for developing the person in work. ❏

6. How do you ensure continuous development through the appraisal?
   a) By looking for areas where they would benefit from developing further ❏
   b) By identifying if there is anything they are no good at ❏
   c) By asking them if they want to do any courses ❏
   d) You only do this with really bright sparks. ❏

7. What do you record in an appraisal?
   a) Whatever the form requires ❏
   b) Achievements and areas for development, with action plans ❏
   c) As little as possible ❏
   d) Everything that is said ❏

8. How do you produce an appraisal framework?
a) We make a recording form. ❏
b) We don't have to do anything – that's HR's job. ❏
c) We collate information on the process and what will be appraised. ❏
d) We don't need a framework – it is in our head. ❏

9. How do you use the framework for appraisal?
a) To guide us and the person being appraised in our preparation ❏
b) To satisfy HR requirements ❏
c) To prove we've done it ❏
d) To record the appraisal ❏

10. Who is the framework for appraisal for?
a) It is for the HR department. ❏
b) It is for us and those who are being appraised. ❏
c) It is just for show. ❏
d) Our bosses like us to have them. ❏

SUNDAY

MONDAY

TUESDAY

WEDNESDAY

THURSDAY

FRIDAY

SATURDAY

# TUESDAY

## The appraiser's role, I: setting the framework

In this chapter, we will begin to look at exactly what your role should be as an appraiser if you want to appraise effectively. We will look at the different elements of general preparation, which will help to make the appraisal itself work well.

Most employees are unclear about what is expected of them in appraisals, so if you brief the employee to be appraised properly, you make it easier for them to play their part. This briefing consists firstly of explaining clearly what the purpose of the appraisal is, for both them and you, and what the principles of the appraisal process are, so that they know why and how they are being appraised. You also need to clarify and agree the actual procedure for the appraisal, and brief them on the preparation they need to do, so that they come to the appraisal ready to play their part.

Finally, you need to do your own preparation specific to the appraisee, collecting evidence of their progress over the year, and looking at what they might usefully develop further, from your point of view. Let's look at what will help you to do this.

# Clarifying the basis for appraisal

It is not enough to sort out for yourself what the purpose of appraisal is, and what criteria you will use.

We have all been in the situation where the other person thought it was obvious why something was important, but we didn't grasp it at all. In that situation, we just feel frustrated and confused.

So don't take it for granted that the person being appraised will see appraisals as valuable, or that they will understand the framework of criteria you are using. The basic rule is: *explain and make explicit.*

This will make your life easier because it will ensure that you are both 'singing from the same hymn sheet'. It will also enable the person being appraised to come prepared with relevant information, examples and ideas. So how do you start?

First of all, you need to spell out the purpose of the appraisal, as in the example below.

### Example

'Appraisals are intended to monitor your (the employee's) performance at work in a constructive way. They provide an opportunity to:

● review what you have been doing and how you have been doing it
● discuss any issues you have which you think may be slowing down your progress, and find ways of dealing with them.

They give you (the employee) the opportunity to:

- give evidence of your achievements and progress, and receive recognition and support for these
- be reminded of how you are contributing to the effectiveness of the whole organization
- voice your views and offer constructive suggestions on both your own development and that of the organization.

Finally, in the appraisal, we can agree together what goals for development you are going to set yourself for the next appraisal and how they can be achieved.'

You could adapt this to your own style, and perhaps even produce it as a written document to give to the individual as reinforcement after you have read it out and checked it through with them.

Next, you need to emphasize the principles of the appraisal and the way in which it will be handled. Remember that most people have a negative experience of performance reviews. From schooldays onwards, when someone 'in authority' comments on our work, it is generally to judge and criticize.

So you need to state clearly and explicitly that an appraisal:

- is a two-way process
- is intended to be useful and constructive
- will recognize positively what the person has achieved
- will help to identify how that person can develop further.

You should also point out clearly that their involvement and contributions are vital to the success of the appraisal.

Third, you need to make explicit what is being appraised and why. The guidelines in the previous chapter will help you and them to understand this.

Finally, they need to be clear that feedback from others is for them to use as part of their evidence on their performance, and that this information will help both of you to identify achievements as well as areas for development. Its purpose is to enhance the information available, not to criticize.

It will take a little time to make sure that these foundations for a successful appraisal are understood and agreed with the person being appraised. This time is well spent, as it is fulfilling a part of your role as appraiser. You are giving the individual the information they need to take an active and constructive part in the appraisal process. By empowering them in this way, you are laying the groundwork to make the appraisal itself more focused, purposeful and productive.

# Agreeing procedures and responsibilities for appraisal

Having clarified the general principles we will be working to in appraisal, we now need to make clear the procedures for appraisal.

## 1 Setting a time for the appraisal interview

To reinforce the statement that appraisals are important and useful, we need to demonstrate that we take them seriously by the way we set them up.

### a The interviews are given a definite time slot in the diary

Most appraisal interviews are held at six-monthly or yearly intervals. They therefore have a lot of ground to cover, and require about 2 hours to be useful. This time needs to be clearly allocated.

### b The time fixed for the appraisal interview is given priority in the diaries of both parties

It is no good saying that your employee must keep this date and time clear if you then cancel because you have an urgent report to write!

As managers, we must set the example of treating appraisals as an important part of our business by keeping to the set time unless we are really forced to change it. Appraisal interviews cannot just be 'fitted in' if they are to be taken seriously.

It may be worth setting aside a set period in the week or month just for appraisal interviews, so that they become a fixture in your calendar.

### c We need to fix the time well enough in advance to give our employees time to prepare properly for the interview

We want our employees to come to the interview well prepared. That means that they need time to review their own performance, and think about their evidence and examples.

If we only give them a day's notice, we are implying that their own review is not that important – assuming they are busy in their job role.

Sometimes, the dates for appraisals are set months in advance. In this case, it is useful to remind your employee a couple of weeks before the date, so that they remember to do their preparation – and likewise yourself.

## 2 Agreeing what preparation the appraisee needs to do

There are several approaches we can take to support the person being appraised in their preparation. It is not enough to give them time and prior warning. They also need some guidelines as to what you mean by preparation.

It can be useful to ask them to make notes, and to offer them a recording sheet which prompts useful evidence and ideas. If you use a recording sheet, it is important that you make clear to them that it is for their benefit and use, not for your records.

Otherwise, a preparation checklist can be useful, leaving them to make notes in their own way.

Before you ask them to record anything, it is important to restate what exactly you want from them. You may choose to use your own version of the following:

---

### Purpose of record

1 To gather evidence to present at appraisal:
  a of own achievements on targets agreed last time
  b of own progress on targets agreed last time
  c of own achievement and progress on other steps towards the goal(s)
2 To remind yourself of any problems you encountered, why you think the problems occurred, and any solutions to the problems which you thought of and/or applied
3 To remind yourself of areas:
  a in which you would benefit from more training
  b in which you would benefit from further practice
  c you would like to pursue further
  d on which you would like to concentrate
4 To remind yourself of anything which felt really good – where you felt pleased with your own learning, or where you felt that the methods used to help you learn were particularly effective
5 To note anything else you might want to say at appraisal
  This is your personal record of your progress towards your goals. It is an *aide-memoire* to help you to contribute as effectively as possible towards your own appraisal.

---

Without the above reminder, you may well forget what you wanted to say, particularly if your appraiser is more confident than you in the process.

But *you* know more than anyone else about your own progress – so don't miss the chance to use that information.

If you would like to give them a recording sheet to use, something like the following can be useful:

---

### Record for appraisee

Tasks done (to remind you of what you've been working on)

Training/teaching received (to remind you of what you've been offered help in, by whom, and how useful it was)

Steps towards goals achieved since last appraised

Steps towards goals made progress in (refer to your copy of the last appraisal record to identify relevant areas)

Areas where problems arose (suggest solutions as well if possible)

Areas you would like to work on next (may be for any of the reasons listed in purpose of recording)

Other comments (anything you would like to say about your progress generally)

---

Extra suggestions for preparation which you can make are:

● That they bring with them supporting evidence, e.g. the first set of minutes they've ever written, a letter from a customer they found difficult to deal with, the end-of-module comments from their college tutor.
   This will give you the opportunity to give specific acknowledgement on things in which they have done well.
   It will also mean that you can discuss specifically with them areas they are finding difficult.
● That they ask for feedback on their performance from others – colleagues, other managers, customers, trainers.

Often we don't know what others think of our performance, and their viewpoint can be very useful information.

Do stress that this is for *their* information, and it is up to them to use it constructively.

This may seem like an awful lot to get across to someone, 'just for an appraisal'.

It is worth noticing that:

- It is only on the first occasion that it takes a long time – after that, you just need to remind them.
- Most people will respond very positively to such clear guidelines, and will take on responsibility for preparing thereafter because they see how useful it is to them.
- You are empowering the person being appraised to take responsibility for making the appraisal useful and focused.
- The act of preparing is in itself a development exercise. It is teaching the individual to review their own performance, to learn from that, and to identify how they could improve.
- The preparation will help the individual to be realistic about the appraisal. They will come to the interview confident of their own ability and progress and/or aware of their need to improve and in what areas.

# Explaining and actioning your preparation

If, as managers, we go through the preparatory work with the person being appraised, we have made our own preparation for the actual appraisal interview much easier. However, some preparation still remains to be done.

## a Read through the previous appraisal record

This will remind us of the targets we agreed with the individual and the areas in which they had progressed at their last review.

## b Gather information from other sources

There may be obvious points we need to follow up on: Did they complete that training programme? How did that project go?

It is useful and constructive to find out factual information before the interview.

If you have not asked the appraisee to get feedback from others, you may wish to consult with their peers, subordinates and customers.

Be careful how you ask about their performance, to elicit clear and specific information.

Examples of useful questions:

- Jack wanted to develop his skills in ... In what ways do you think he is progressing? Are there any ways in which you think his development could be increased?
- Can you give me any examples where Jill has shown good progress while doing ... ? Can you give me any areas where you think she could progress more quickly by approaching it a different way?
- If I ask you to summarize Jack's progress over the last month in relation to his goals, what would you say?

> It is important to remind people of what the criteria for development are: Jack may be pleasant to work with, but may not have improved his carpentry skills at all.

## c Consider your own view of their performance and collect your own evidence

You can use the same checklist as they use, and can also make brief notes throughout the year of things you notice, so that the information is already there. This helps us to consider the whole period, rather than just focusing on something that happened last week.

## d Clarify for yourself what results you want from this appraisal

This will remind you to:

- apply the principles of appraisal
- refer to the business goals and refresh your awareness of them
- refer to their job specification
- focus your attention on learning and development rather than faults.

It is important that you tell the person being appraised that you are doing this preparation.

They will then know that you are taking the appraisal seriously. They will also know that you will have a great deal of information on them to hand, which will encourage them to make more effort to gather relevant information also.

Finally, it is important to timetable sufficient space for you to do this preparation. You can use the same device you used for the person being appraised to prompt yourself into allocating specific time for information gathering.

## Explaining how the interview will proceed

We all tend to get rather nervous about 'interviews', however well we know and get on with the interviewer. It is made easier if we know beforehand the structure of the interview and the approach to be used. We will discuss this in detail in later chapters.

You need to clarify your approach and the structure you will use, and then ensure that you explain this to the person being appraised beforehand.

To a large extent, this is implicit in all the explanations you have given them so far. It is, however, still worth making explicit, so that you are sure that they really do understand how the interview will be run.

# Summary

We have explored how you can use your own thinking-through of the purpose and principles of appraisal to explain them to those you will appraise, so that they are also clear about why and how appraisals will be conducted. We have also explored ways of helping them to fulfil their part in the appraisal effectively, so that it really is a two-way process, by giving them useful guidelines and by clarifying with them the preparation they need to do.

Finally, we have also looked at what you need to do specifically for each person you appraise, so that you are well informed and well prepared for the interview.

Although all this may seem time-consuming, it is important to recognize that:

● It makes a considerable difference to the effectiveness of the appraisal itself, enabling both you and the person being appraised to be ready to use the opportunity well.
● Much of it is a one-off activity. Once you have prepared the briefing on the purpose and principles of appraisal, and the procedures and responsibilities, these can be used with all your employees and will only need the briefest of reviews, to check they are still valid, in following years.

The following multiple-choice questions are a reminder of what we've covered today.

SUNDAY
MONDAY
TUESDAY
WEDNESDAY
THURSDAY
FRIDAY
SATURDAY

# Questions (answers at the back)

1. Why do we need to explain to the person being appraised what appraisals are all about?
a) Because we cannot take it for granted that they understand their importance and relevance. ❑
b) We only need to if they haven't been appraised before. ❑
c) Because the forms are complicated. ❑
d) Because it's part of the process. ❑

2. How do you start to explain about appraisals?
a) By showing them the forms ❑
b) By giving them the guidance document ❑
c) By talking about the purpose of appraisals ❑
d) By telling them they have to do them ❑

3. Why do we emphasize the principles of appraisal?
a) Because it's part of the process ❑
b) Because they make explicit the constructive nature of appraisals ❑
c) Because then they will know what to do ❑
d) Because principles matter ❑

4. What procedures do we need to explain to the person being appraised?
a) The timing of appraisals and their priority in the diary ❑

b) What HR needs from the appraisal ❑
c) That we fit in appraisals when we're not too busy ❑
d) That we'll complete the forms ❑

5. How do we help the person being appraised to prepare?
a) We give them a recording form. ❑
b) We tell them to collect evidence for themselves. ❑
c) We just tell them to be prepared. ❑
d) We give them information about what to collect as their evidence. ❑

6. Why is it important to take the time to go through all the information with people?
a) It only matters if they haven't done one before. ❑
b) It empowers them to make the best use of their appraisal. ❑
c) They might not get it right otherwise. ❑
d) It means they can't complain that they haven't been informed. ❑

7. What other preparation do you need to do for yourself?
a) Recall the mistakes they've made. ❑
b) Think of something nice to say. ❑
c) Collect your own information on their performance. ❑
d) Get out last year's appraisal record. ❑

8. What do you do to ensure that you approach your preparation in the right way?
a) I remind myself of the purpose and principles of appraisal. ❏
b) I read last year's appraisal record. ❏
c) I cushion the negative with a positive. ❏
d) I give it a bit of time. ❏

9. When do you do your preparation?
a) Just before the appraisal ❏
b) When I can fit it in ❏
c) In advance, with time allocated in my diary ❏
d) When I see the appraisal interview slot in my diary ❏

10. Why do we spend time on all this preparation?
a) HR thinks it's important. ❏
b) It makes the appraisal itself much more valuable and useful. ❏
c) Because we're supposed to. ❏
d) I wish I knew! ❏

SUNDAY

MONDAY

TUESDAY

WEDNESDAY

THURSDAY

FRIDAY

SATURDAY

# WEDNESDAY

## The appraiser's role, II: attitudes and approaches

We have looked at the practical preparation that you need to do as an appraiser, but that is not the only preparation needed for the appraisal to be effective. Just as important is the way you prepare yourself and think through your attitude and approach to the appraisal interview. How we are with the person being appraised affects how they play their part in the appraisal.

In this chapter, we will consider how you can prepare yourself to approach the interview constructively and sympathetically, making sure that you set yourself up usefully and set the right tone in the interview. We will also look at how you can establish trust between yourself and your employee in the interview, so that they feel more comfortable.

Finally, we will consider the important behaviours you need to adopt, so that the appraisal interview really works, including gathering as much information as possible from the employee, listening with proper attention to what they have to say, encouraging them to take more responsibility for their own development, and coming to genuine agreement about the conclusions drawn in the interview. This way you will have a genuinely useful two-way conversation.

# Being ready

We often find that we come into another meeting carrying with us the pressures of previous and following activities. Although we intend to give the meeting our full attention, the fact is that our minds are elsewhere.

It only takes a few minutes to set your 'baggage' aside, relax, and focus on the meeting you are about to go into. This will help you to pay full attention in the way in which the person being appraised deserves.

We also need to realize that, as appraiser, you can feel as tense and nervous about the interview as the person being appraised. You want it to go well, and be useful, but you may be new to the role, or you may be unsure about your credibility as an appraiser.

If this is the case, remember the following:

- This is not a test for either side, it's a joint venture, with both of you wanting it to be useful.
- The person being appraised will be more nervous than you; concentrate on making them feel alright and you will automatically ease down yourself.
- Take a few deep breaths before you start, and consciously relax muscular tension; if you can physically relax, you will be more able to perform well.

- If you admit to being a bit nervous about it to the person being appraised, they will think more of you, not less; it makes them feel less 'unique' in being nervous, it establishes something in common, and it means that they will understand if you want to rephrase a question or correct some statement that you feel isn't quite 'in the right spirit'.

Do glance at your preparation notes just to remind yourself of your focus.

**Checklist: being ready**

- *Take a few minutes to separate yourself from previous activities and ones which you have to do afterwards.*
- *Take a couple of deep breaths and relax.*
- *Glance at your preparation notes.*

# Establishing trust

We need to ensure that the person being appraised feels safe and relaxed, in order to get the best out of the appraisal interview.

The preparation we have done with them will have established some of the trusting relationship we need in order to make the appraisal interview useful. However, we still need to make sure they feel that we are 'on their side'. The actual interview often brings out more anxiety and more formality on both sides.

We establish trust in a variety of ways:

- Make the environment comfortable and relaxed; also ensure that the interview takes place somewhere where you cannot be overheard and will not be interrupted.
- Greet them by name, in a friendly manner (the first impression always has an impact).
- Make a little 'small talk' before you start straight into the interview; it reminds you that you are both ordinary human beings, not just appraiser and appraisee.

- Remind the appraisee of the purpose of the appraisal interview, and the structure; this sets the tone and reminds you both that you are working together to achieve a useful end result.
- State explicitly that anything said or discussed within the interview is just between the two of you; if anything is raised which requires discussion with a third party, then you need to agree with them how that will be done.
- Check that your body language matches what you are saying; we all know instinctively when someone is only saying what we want to hear.

Remember that these ways of establishing trust are only the starting point. You need to follow them through in practice, so that the person being appraised knows that they are genuine.

This means:

- Don't allow interruptions.
- Greet that person in a friendly manner at times other than the appraisal interview.
- Take a few minutes to chat to them in the workplace as well.
- Make sure the whole interview fulfils its purpose.
- Maintain confidentiality.
- Remember to keep yourself open and positive.

We none of us trust someone who turns their demonstration of trustworthiness off and on with us. We are suspicious of them if they suddenly become positive and supportive in a particular situation, and don't believe that it is genuine.

> Establishing trust is a continuous process, not just a set of behaviours to be 'switched on' for appraisal.

## Finding out

An important part of what you need to do as appraiser is to gather useful information from the appraisee. Once you have established some trust, they are more likely to give you genuine information, rather than saying what they think you want to hear.

For an appraisal to be useful, you need to be very clear about the appraisee's view of things, what makes *them* feel they've achieved or progressed, where *they* think they need help or improvement. All too often we impose our own view. Although the other person may go along with us, it rarely results in the effect we want because it's not quite the same as their view, so they are less committed to it.

> *'To be complimented for excellent completion of my administrative tasks may be nice, but why wasn't my representation at the regional meeting noticed?'*

> *'To have suggested that a counselling skills course may be useful is accurate, but right now I'd prefer to improve my computing skills.'*

We have asked the appraisee to prepare by bringing examples of their own. It is vital that we give value to that preparation, and use it as the starting point for the appraisal.

We need first to find out what they have prepared. Simple questions are required here:

'What do you think are your achievements?'

Then we need to ensure that we have really understood what their example means to them. Our normal task would be to ask why that is an achievement. This is less useful than the following questions:

'In what way do you see that as an achievement?'

'What specifically makes you feel that is an achievement?'

We then have both the example and the opinion of the individual. We can now give appropriate recognition.

Notice that at first an individual may only give one or two examples, and we may need to prompt them for more. Questions such as:

'What else do you think of as an achievement?'

'How else have you progressed?'

will tempt them into giving more examples.

In the same vein, we can find out what they think their obstacles to progress are.

'What do you think is stopping you progressing?'

'And what else?'

Finally, we want to find out what they think would enable them to progress and develop. We may have our own ideas, but theirs need to be explored first. We all prefer to implement our own solutions. So we need to ask questions like:

'How would you change this?'

'What do you think would help you to overcome this?'

'What would help you to develop this?'

Notice the common themes of these questions. They all start with 'what' or 'how' and they all ask the person to express their own view – 'what do you think ...'.

There may be information which you have which suggests something different from what they say.

- You may have something else which you consider to be improvement or progress; you can now add that to their own list, so it is a bonus not a replacement.
- You may have other areas of concern; you need to explain how they are a concern, how they relate to business or personal targets, and again ask the interviewee for their opinion and their ideas of how to deal with it.
- You may have different proposals for development or next targets; you can now suggest yours, as additional possibilities – however, what is finally agreed will be from the choice of their ideas and yours, not exclusively yours.

It is often the case that the appraisee covers all the ground you have thought of, and sometimes more. If they are allowed to tell you, rather than you tell them, they are far more likely to act on it.

You are the reinforcer, recognizer, supporter and helper, rather than the dictator.

# Listening

In order to find out someone's viewpoint effectively, we need to listen with full attention. This means that we listen, not just to what they say but also to how they say it.

- Do they sound confident or doubting?
- Are they hesitating or in full throttle?
- Does their body language match what they are saying?

Listening with full attention means listening with our ears, our eyes, our hearts and our intuition. And when you notice something which doesn't quite fit, ask about it. Possible questions might be:

'You seem unsure/pleased/worried/certain about that. What makes you that way?'

'How does that affect you?'

We can often save ourselves a lot of time and energy by listening with full attention. It helps us to spot quickly what is important in the communication.

Moreover, being a good listener is a quality which others really appreciate, and it helps to enhance the relationship.

# Empowering

We want the person being appraised to take on more and more responsibility for their own development. For this to happen, they need to feel empowered to do so.

Empowerment has three main components:

1 reinforcing and encouraging the taking on of responsibility
2 giving clear and useful information
3 valuing the person's own thoughts, opinions and suggestions.

Much of what we have described so far has this effect:

- giving them a clear purpose and framework for the appraisal
- asking them to prepare clear guidelines
- taking their preparation and examples first, before offering your own.

All the time, we need to bear in mind that we want them to decide for themselves, rather than imposing decisions on them. So you need to give them a lot of encouragement in the first place.

Statements that start with the following are useful:

'I think it's excellent that you ...'
'I like the way you ...'
'I'm pleased that you ...'
'I'm impressed that you ...'

We often think these things, even say them to other people, but don't remember to say them to the person concerned!

However, don't make such remarks unless they are genuine, otherwise the person may feel that you are trying to con them.

If you do feel that you have to impose a decision, make it clear why. By giving explicit information, you reduce the disempowering effect. Also notice that often, if you give them the information you have, they will make the decision for you anyway.

**Example**

'I have just had my budget for external training cut, so I will not be able to fund all the programmes my staff might want, and will have to find alternative methods for development. How else could we tackle this area of development which you are asking for?'

Finally, you may find that you don't fully agree with the individual's view of progress, priorities, etc.

Distinguish between your own preferences and those in the best interests of the business.

We often encourage people to agree with our personal view, as if it is factually better. We may think it is, but we need to remember that people do things they have chosen for themselves more wholeheartedly.

Wherever possible, let the person choose their own priorities. They may then be more open to your suggestions next time.

# Negotiating and agreeing

There are often areas of the appraisal where there is some difference of opinion. Your role is to find a way of coming to an agreement, rather than standing your ground.

When we encounter this situation with friends, we usually handle it well: we may give some ground, and in return they give some, until we find something which suits us both and takes us both towards the result we want.

Use the same approach in an appraisal interview.

It is guaranteed that you both want the individual to perform to their optimum potential. The difference may be in how you think that will be achieved.

Anything which is a step towards that is useful, so, be flexible in your negotiating and accept the possibility of alternatives. Unless the person can genuinely agree to the targets, you will not get the results you want.

# Summary

In this chapter, we have looked at the approach you need to take in order for an appraisal interview to be useful, and the importance of this personal preparation. We have emphasized the fact that you set the tone for the interview, and that your attitude and approach will make all the difference to how it goes. None of this is rocket science, just good sense if we want any interaction to go well.

We often forget that how we behave has a significant effect on the way the other person responds to us, because we are busy getting on with the task in hand.

This form of preparation is not time-consuming – it only takes a few minutes to sort yourself out before you enter the interaction. Above all, remember that this is another human being in front of you, with their own particular mix of strengths and weaknesses, and that, more than anything, they want to feel valued for what they do well, and supported in developing themselves.

And, if you are unsure of what to say or how to react, just think how you would prefer to be treated if you were sitting in their chair – that is usually a useful guide.

The following multiple-choice questions are a reminder of what we've covered today.

SUNDAY

MONDAY

TUESDAY

WEDNESDAY

THURSDAY

FRIDAY

SATURDAY

# Questions (answers at the back)

1. How do you make sure you are ready to pay attention before the appraisal interview?
   a) I tell myself I need to pay attention. ❏
   b) I try and time it for first thing in the morning or last thing in the day. ❏
   c) I take a few minutes to relax and set my baggage aside. ❏
   d) I always pay attention. ❏

2. What do you do if you feel a bit nervous before the appraisal interview?
   a) I won't feel nervous. ❏
   b) I remember this is not a test for either side and take a deep breath. ❏
   c) I hide it from the person being appraised. ❏
   d) I dismiss it as irrelevant. ❏

3. Why do we need to establish trust in the interview?
   a) The trust will already be there. ❏
   b) To draw out the truth from them ❏
   c) Because they're bound to be nervous ❏
   d) To ensure the person being appraised feels safe and relaxed ❏

4. How can we establish trust at the beginning of the interview?
   a) Tell them they can trust us. ❏
   b) Say something nice to them. ❏
   c) Give them something to drink. ❏
   d) Greet them by name in a friendly manner and state confidentiality. ❏

5. What makes establishing trust in the interview easier?
   a) Being equally friendly and open during the year ❏
   b) If I know them well ❏
   c) If they've worked for me for a long time ❏
   d) Not sitting behind my desk ❏

6. How do we find out what they think they have achieved?
   a) By asking them if they agree with our opinion ❏
   b) By asking them open questions which prompt them to give their evidence ❏
   c) We both already know what they've achieved. ❏
   d) By asking them what they've done ❏

7. How do we give our opinion of their progress and performance?
   a) We tell them what we think. ❏
   b) We read out our assessment of them. ❏
   c) By reinforcing their points and adding our own ❏
   d) By our attitude to their evidence ❏

8. What do we need to listen to during the appraisal interview?
a) Not just what they say, but how they say it ❏
b) What they think they've done ❏
c) Their comments on our assessment of them ❏
d) Their opinion ❏

9. How do we empower them during the appraisal interview?
a) By telling them they are empowered ❏
b) Appraisal interviews aren't where empowerment happens. ❏
c) We let them have their say. ❏
d) By encouraging them to decide for themselves what will work best for them ❏

10. How do we set targets for them in the appraisal interview?
a) We tell them their targets. ❏
b) By negotiating with them and finding genuine agreement ❏
c) By referring to their job description ❏
d) By picking up on what they've failed in ❏

SUNDAY

MONDAY

TUESDAY

WEDNESDAY

THURSDAY

FRIDAY

SATURDAY

# THURSDAY

# The interview, I: reviewing achievement

Having prepared both the appraisee and yourself, it is now time to conduct the actual appraisal interview. In this chapter, we will begin to explore how you structure the appraisal interview, so that you have useful results.

Firstly, we will look at how you agree an overall agenda for the interview, so you are both clear about what you are doing. We also suggest that you agree the outcomes of the interview, so you are both clear about what you are trying to achieve.

Then we will explore how you can conduct the review part of the appraisal. In this, we look at how to use previous targets as the focus for review, and how to review when there are no previous targets, in an initial appraisal. We will look at how you ensure that your employee feels that they have been recognized and valued for progress and achievement, as this is the main purpose of the review stage. Then we look at how you handle a lack of progress and/or achievement in a constructive way.

# Agreeing overall agenda and outcomes

In a formal business meeting, we usually have an agenda. We often forget to set an agenda for other meetings.

It helps to have something which gives a framework to the appraisal interview, and also links in to the amount of time available for it. This will enable you both to keep on track and stay focused.

---

**Appraisal Agenda**

| | |
|---|---|
| 9.30 | Review of previous appraisal and agreed action therein |
| 9.45 | Discussion of general progress and achievements |
| 10.00 | Identification and discussion of organizational issues |
| 10.15 | Identification of areas for further development or support |
| 10.35 | Coffee break |
| 10.50 | Agreement of an action plan |
| 11.15 | Recording of agreed outcomes and new targets |
| | Confirmation of date for next appraisal |

---

Equipped with a plan of this kind, having greeted the person being appraised, we can start by agreeing the agenda with them.

It is also well worth explicitly agreeing with them the outcomes you both want from the interview. These might be such things as:

- that both feel it has been a constructive meeting
- that recognition has been given to achievement and progress
- that realistic targets have been agreed, with appropriate action to be undertaken on both sides.

# Agreeing achievement and progress

The first stage of any appraisal is the recognition of achievement and progress.

## Referring to targets

We have two ways of focusing on this area, depending on whether this is a first or repeated appraisal. In the latter case, we start by referring to targets set in the previous appraisal.
  We might ask:

'What progress do you feel you have made against the targets agreed last time?'

'What examples/evidence can you mention to support this?'

We can then broaden the base beyond these targets to ask:

'In what other areas do you think you have progressed?'

'What else do you feel you have achieved?'

  It is then appropriate to give due recognition for their examples, and add any further examples you have collected.

It can be helpful to ask a further question, to get some sense of their priorities:

'Which of these are you most proud of/pleased with?'

As they give you this information, remember to:

- ensure that you have understood fully their example/ evidence
- give value/recognition to their examples/evidence
- add to their list where you can, or certainly endorse it from your own information gathering
- encourage them to link achievements and progress to both business and personal objectives.

In this part of the process, you will need to begin to record the examples. However, beware: we often get so caught up in writing notes, that we don't give the appraisee our full attention.

It may be useful to have some scrap paper, and say to the person being appraised that you are just going to jot down a key word or phrase to remind you both of the achievement and progress covered.

Then, when you have covered all the areas of achievement and progress, use your notes to review them, and agree what should be written on the appraisal record. Completing it there and then, and showing it to the interviewee, also helps to build trust. A by-product is that it saves time afterwards.

## Initial appraisal

On an initial appraisal, there are no previous targets to review. What is more, the interview often takes place soon after someone has started in their job, and they may feel that they have no significant achievement or progress to report.

We need to remember that this appraisal will set the tone for subsequent ones.

So, make sure you:

- go through the same preparatory process with the person
- ask them to produce their evidence, but give them the freedom to bring evidence from previous employment or other life experience as well

- do start with achievements and progress as the first area to focus on, and give recognition
- add in the achievement of getting the job and settling in.

## What if someone doesn't feel they have progressed or achieved anything?

Do try to find some areas of progress. Sometimes people have very high expectations of themselves, and we can help them to recognize steps taken towards what they want to achieve, which they have dismissed as 'not enough'.

## What if you don't think someone has progressed or achieved anything?

Again, do try to find something which can genuinely be seen as progress, as in the case above.

Are you expecting too much? As much as we can, we want to recognize achievement and progress, however small it may be. We then have something to build on for the next targets.

We all know how awful it feels to have failed utterly. That is not a good point from which to start looking at how to improve. At the very least, everyone can learn something from a failure; it's the first step forward.

Only as a last resort are we going to agree with someone that they have achieved nothing and made no progress. And if that happens, we need to question ourselves as well. How could we let that happen and have done nothing about it until now?

# Dealing constructively with lack of achievement

Having established some recognition for progress and achievement, we now need to deal with the second area of focus: where someone hasn't achieved or progressed.

## Referring to targets

Again, we start by reviewing the targets set at the last appraisal, to discover if there are any which have not been met.

We need to be careful with our questions about a lack of achievement. It is very easy to make someone defensive, despite our best intentions. They will already feel disappointed themselves, so we need to be constructive with them, to help them find ways of overcoming it.

Useful questions might be:

● What targets have you not achieved?
● What have you achieved towards those targets?
● What stopped you from achieving them?
● What would help you to achieve them now?

Having listened carefully to the responses, we can:

● endorse any progress towards targets, however small
● add further suggestions for what might help.

Often, people will blame the organization, or other people. They feel they have become a 'victim of circumstance'.

There is usually some degree of truth in this, and it is important to take account of it. You may be able to help make a difference, say by agreeing to a change of priorities in the job description and telling their supervisor. Or you may agree with them that the recent increased workload made the target unrealistic.

However, it is important to help them to identify some means of taking hold of the situation for themselves, so that they feel empowered rather than victimized.

Maybe they could talk directly to the colleague who is constantly interrupting them with queries. Maybe they could reorganize their workload themselves to give some regular time to a particular target area.

The question to ask, if they are feeling powerless to change the situation, is:

'And what can you do to help yourself to achieve this?'

Remember the result you want from this appraisal interview: a member of staff who feels valued for what they have achieved, capable of continuing to improve, and motivated to work on their own continuing development.

We want to reinforce their own ability to make a difference, not their failure to do so.

We may need to work with them for a while in the area of constructive ways of dealing with a lack of achievement.

Most of us are knocked back by failure, and become either defensive or helpless. We need to help our staff to feel safe in admitting to a failure, and positive about looking at alternatives.

It can be useful to remind someone that, as a small child trying to walk, they didn't say 'It's not fair', or give up, if they fell on their

bottoms. They just got up and tried again, often in a different way, with more support from the furniture, until they could walk easily. The same principle applies to any personal development.

## Different approaches you might use

### 1 If their intended achievement or target was a large 'chunk'

An example might be: 'I want to revise all of my admin procedures, but I've only started on one or two.'

Help them to break the target down into more realistic steps which they can achieve. Separate out the different parts which need revision, or stages of revision.

### 2 If their intended achievement target was too vaguely expressed.

An example might be: 'I want to improve my relations with other staff, but it's not really working.'

Help them to make it more specific: with whom and in what way, and how will they know when they have?

### 3 If they are lacking the confidence to get started

An example might be: 'I want to express my opinions at staff meetings, but I feel nervous of looking stupid.'

Talk through with them what kinds of things they might want to express an opinion about, such as items on a staff meeting agenda. Ask them what they would like to say and how, so they have 'rehearsed' it. Offer them your support and encouragement to do it at the next meeting.

### 4 If they have a specific difficulty

An example might be: 'I want to learn word processing, and I started the evening class, but then missed four sessions because of illness in the family and I can't catch up.'

Explore with them possible ways past the difficulty, and look at alternatives with them. In this instance options might include extra lessons, a different learning route, such as Open Learning, help from a colleague, etc.

Our intention is always to help them learn and move on from a lack of achievement or progress. As we continue to deal with the individual's feeling of failure in this constructive way, they will:

- be more honest about talking about their lack of achievement
- begin to be more constructive themselves in finding ways to have another go.

## Going beyond targets

So far, we have focused on lack of achievement or progress against targets. There may, however, be other areas where someone feels that their achievement or progress has been blocked. It is important to open up the discussion on these, because they are likely to be significant to the individual. You may use the question:

'Is there any other area in which you feel you have not progressed as you would have liked?'

We can then use the same approach as for those areas identified against targets.

## What if you think there are other areas where there is a lack of achievement or progress?

If the appraisee has identified relatively few, then it may be useful to add in a couple. Make sure in each case that you explain very clearly in what way you consider there to be a lack of progress, and be careful not to expect too much of the individual.

It is important to weigh up how important your identified areas are to the business. We want to maintain, wherever possible, an emphasis on the positive and constructive.

Could these areas be used as part of the appraisee's general development plan, rather than used to highlight a lack of progress?

# What if someone thinks they have no areas where there is a lack of achievement or progress?

We want to set the tone of continuous improvement, so we can delight in the lack of gaps and, at the same time, look for areas for development, which is much more positive. We might ask:

'In which areas of your work would you like to develop further? How?'

## Initial appraisal

Obviously, in an initial appraisal, there can be no lack of progress or achievement.

We can therefore go straight to the positive tone of development, as set out above. This reminds both manager and newcomer that part of the purpose of appraisal will always be to encourage continuous improvement.

## Recording the interview

While discussing this part of the appraisal, it is again important to make brief notes of areas raised and possible action to take.

These can be summarized and recorded, with the agreement of the person being appraised.

# Summary

We have been looking at how you start the appraisal interview, to set the right tone, and then how you conduct the first part of the appraisal interview, the review stage, emphasizing the positive and constructive. It is vital that the person being appraised feels valued and supported, and that you encourage them to play their part fully.

It reminds us that the appraisal interview is dependent on the preparation by both parties that we have suggested. It also demonstrates that the appraisal interview is just a summary point for the previous year, in the review stage, and is much easier to do if you have kept regular contact with the person, to check on their progress during the year. It is an opportunity to give recognition to what people have done and how they have done it. It is the link point between the previous year and what progress, achievement and development can happen in the next year.

When reviewing, above all, remember to set a positive and constructive tone. This genuinely gives the person the sense that you want them to do well and recognize the value of what they have done, as well as being ready to support their development.

The following multiple-choice questions are a reminder of what we've covered today.

SUNDAY
MONDAY
TUESDAY
WEDNESDAY
THURSDAY
FRIDAY
SATURDAY

# Questions (answers at the back)

1. What is an appraisal agenda?
   a) A timetabled structure for the interview ❏
   b) My plan for the appraisal ❏
   c) A day of appraisals in my diary ❏
   d) We don't need an agenda for appraisals. ❏

2. How do you set the outcomes for the appraisal interview?
   a) By deciding on them beforehand ❏
   b) The outcome is just a completed appraisal record. ❏
   c) By agreeing them at the beginning with the person being appraised ❏
   d) By asking the person being appraised what they want out of it ❏

3. How do you use previous targets or objectives?
   a) To remind me what I asked them to do ❏
   b) To establish what progress the person has made ❏
   c) To check what they've not achieved ❏
   d) To fill in the first part of the appraisal record ❏

4. How do you verify their progress?
   a) By questioning them hard on what they say ❏
   b) By asking them for evidence ❏
   c) By taking their word for it ❏
   d) By checking if I have the same thing on my list ❏

5. What do you need to be aware of when taking notes?
   a) That I need to fill in all the boxes on the appraisal record ❏
   b) That I make sure I get everything written down ❏
   c) That I don't want to have to rewrite it because it's untidy ❏
   d) That I might not pay proper attention to the person being appraised ❏

6. If it is an initial appraisal, how do you review?
   a) I can't do any review until they've been with me for a year. ❏
   b) I ask them how it's going. ❏
   c) By asking them to use previous employment examples ❏
   d) I make something up. ❏

7. What do you do if someone thinks they have not made any progress?
   a) Work with them to find something constructive. ❏
   b) Tell them they need to improve. ❏
   c) Try and make them feel OK about it. ❏
   d) In some jobs, I just don't – there's nothing to progress in. ❏

8. What do you do if they have not achieved their targets?
a) Tell them it's not good enough. ❏
b) Find out what stopped them from achieving them. ❏
c) Set the same targets for next year. ❏
d) Try not to draw attention to it. ❏

9. How do you help them to deal with a feeling of failure?
a) Tell them it happens – live with it. ❏
b) Use that feeling to make them try harder. ❏
c) Feel sorry for them. ❏
d) Help them to see how they could progress from that to development. ❏

10. How do you encourage someone who has achieved all they set out to do to find areas for development?
a) There's no need to. ❏
b) By asking them what they would like to take further ❏
c) By finding something hard for them to do next ❏
d) By telling them what I think they could do that would be development ❏

SUNDAY

MONDAY

TUESDAY

WEDNESDAY

THURSDAY

FRIDAY

SATURDAY

# FRIDAY

## The interview, II: looking ahead

Once we have conducted the review part of the appraisal interview, it is time to look ahead and plan for the next year's development and expected achievements. In this chapter, we will begin by exploring a little more what continuous improvement or development really means, and what we need to do to emphasize its importance.

We will then look at how you set goals and targets, so that they are clearly relevant, actionable and achievable. We look particularly at how you relate them to the review part, and how you encourage the person being appraised to actively contribute. We also look at how you can help them to put their targets and goals into an action plan, prioritizing and organizing them, so they know where to start.

Finally, we look at how you round off the interview in a way that confirms the content you have covered, appreciates the other person's contribution to its success, and reasserts the approach used throughout.

# Continuous improvement and development

Let us pick up this theme from yesterday, and expand on it a little.

All too often an appraisal seems to say either: 'You've done alright, keep going,' or 'You're not good enough, do better.'

Successful appraisals say: 'You've got this far. Now where are you going?' They emphasize development rather than picking up on remedial needs.

When we look at ways of encouraging continuous improvement, we can take it through three stages:

1 improvements which will make it easier for the person concerned to perform well in their job – *job related*
2 improvements which will enable the person to contribute even more effectively to business objectives – *company related*
3 improvements which will develop the person's potential – *person related*.

In the first stage, we are encouraging the individual to look at ways of achieving their peak performance in the specific job which they have.

In the second stage, we are encouraging the individual to develop and demonstrate their potential for wider application. This may also help us to identify potential for promotion or new job roles.

In the third stage, we are encouraging the individual to 'round out' and develop their personal qualities. This, of course, will also benefit them and the company in their work roles.

With these three possible areas for development, no one can say, 'There's nowhere further for me to go.' None of us have finished our development in any of the three, and between them they open up a wide range of possible needs and wants in development.

We want all our staff to be constantly looking for what else and what more they can develop in themselves. This leads not just to successful appraisals, but also to successful organizations.

# Setting goals and targets

To encourage this process of continuous improvement, we need to ensure that the person being appraised sets themselves appropriate goals and targets.

These emerge naturally from the previous sections of the appraisal interview on achievement and progress, areas of difficulty, and desired developments.

It is helpful to structure the formulating of the goals and targets, so that they are usable.

## What are goals and targets?

A goal is the end result that a person wants to achieve. Examples are:

● a further qualification in their subject area
● no work backlog
● more effective staff meetings.

The problem with most goals is that they are fairly large, and often not very clearly defined.

It is important to clarify how you will know if you have achieved the goal, so that you can clarify what exactly it means.

Questions to help you do this might be:

'What evidence will you have that you have achieved your goal?'

'How will you know when you have achieved your goal?'

'What exactly will demonstrate that you have achieved your goal?'

After answering one of these questions, our previous examples of goals would be much clearer:

'I want to improve my skills in my work by taking a further qualification.'

'I want to improve my time management, so that I clear my work to deadline or before. I also want to tackle my present backlog until it is cleared.'

'I want my staff meetings to be shorter and to be fully attended.'

'I want my staff to act on decisions made at the meetings.'

A simple way of getting these fuller statements of goals is to ask people to express them in this format:

'I want to improve ... The result(s) will be ...'

*Targets* are the steps along the way to achieving a goal. Examples are:

- I will enrol in the college course.
- I will timetable my work for the week.
- I will ask my staff what they think would improve the effectiveness of our staff meetings.

Targets need to be kept to a realistic size, so that they are achievable. They also help us to break down the achievement of a goal into small chunks, and to identify exactly what is required of us to achieve that goal. They are the actions we need to take.

To clarify the targets, we might ask:

'What do you need to do to achieve that goal?'

'How will you work towards that goal?'

'What is the first/next step you need to take to achieve that goal?'

It is important to make the targets specific and, where possible, date their completion.

So our examples might become:

'I will enrol in the college course at Smith College by 6th September.'

'I will plan out next week's work in my diary, with blocks of time for different activities.'

'I will put together a simple questionnaire on different aspects of staff meetings to use with my staff by next Friday.'

Now we have something concrete to do, rather than an intention. And we can produce a simple formula to help ourselves and others to set targets:

'I will do ... by ... in this way ...'

## Enabling others to set goals and targets

In the appraisal interview, setting goals and targets is the stage where we begin to pin down the wide-ranging review of past achievements and progress and newly identified areas for development. We want to turn this broad spectrum into a useful and manageable plan for the future.

We have, by this stage, notes on all the areas which have been covered so far by the interview. These notes comprise most of the 'menu' for possible goals and targets. First, they cover all the areas which are seen as important; the individual is far more likely to commit to further development in these areas. Secondly, they cover areas that the interviewee hasn't mentioned, but which we have already noted as important.

The only part of the menu not yet identified is anything which relates to changed or changing business or personal objectives.

For example, if the individual is about to move into a newly formed staff team with different responsibilities, this may throw up some different areas for development, which require goals and targets.

We can usually put all these elements into three areas of goals and targets to consider:

1 those based on a desire for development in areas of progress and achievement

2 those based on need for development in areas where there is a lack of progress or achievement

3 those based on a desire or need for development to accommodate coming changes.

If you have been thorough in the review so far, you may well find that there are a lot of items which could potentially be the subjects of goals and targets.

It is vital that we find a way of narrowing these down to an achievable level. Better to set a limited number of goals and targets, and encourage people to go beyond them, than to cover every area and leave them with so much to achieve that they give up.

How do we do this?

## 1 Sort out the possible goal with the person

Ideally, there would be between three and six goals.

Encourage them to choose their own. If you need to insist on a goal which they are not choosing, then negotiate with them.

For example, if someone is resisting becoming computer literate, and it is important for business objectives that they do take this on, then you may suggest that they take this as one goal, but also agree to their preferred goal of being more active in meetings.

Notice that sometimes the goals will still be the same as at the last appraisal. Someone may be working towards a large goal over quite a long period of time.

## 2 Set up targets within each goal area

Using the formula described above, we can help the individual to sort out their targets, which will be the steps towards the goal.

Again, we need to ensure that these targets are realistically sized chunks, which will help them to notice progress as well as achievement.

If they have not achieved a previous target, beware of setting exactly the same target again. We need to find out what stopped them, and if possible think of an alternative target. We don't want people simply to repeat a failure.

# Action planning

Now we know what the person is wanting to work on during the period before the next appraisal, we need to help them to organize and prioritize those actions, to produce an action plan.

This is a vital part of the motivation of the person. Without it, it is easy to:

- be overwhelmed by the amount you have committed to, and put things off until the last minute
- avoid the areas you have less interest in or motivation towards
- get so involved in one area of development that you go beyond your goals in that, but neglect the other areas.

## How do we action plan?

There are several possible strategies, but the most effective will have the following features:

- The action plan is clear and simple.
- The action points will each have a deadline against them which spreads them across the period.
- In each time period there will be some action points which are easy and pleasing to achieve.
- Major action points will be evenly distributed across the time periods.

To achieve this sorting, it can be useful to use a simple matrix, to begin to classify the action points.

|  | MUST | |
| --- | --- | --- |
| + | | − |
| | Must<br>Want to | Needn't<br>Want to |
| WANT | | |
| | Must<br>Don't want to | Don't need to<br>Don't want to |
| − | | |

> **If any point falls into the bottom right-hand box, then it is questionable whether it is a real target!**

It is important to involve the person being appraised fully in the identification of categories for the action points.

From this, it is easy to put together an action plan which satisfies the effectiveness factors. The person themselves will usually do this part well on their own, if given the guidelines.

An example for a two-month period would be:

---

(M + W = Must + Want to, M = Must, W = Want to)

*By the end of April*

Find out about programmes on counselling available

(M + W)

Produce a new format for monthly reports (M)

Read and pass on the professional magazines which are in my pending tray (W)

---

Reorganize the way I file things in my trays (W)

*By the end of May*

Meet with the training manager to sort out which counselling programme I can attend (M + W)

Introduce the new monthly report format to my staff with an example (M)

Clear three non-urgent items from my filing trays each week (W)

Check and renew the notice board (M + W)

The individual now has their action plan divided into manageable chunks. Targets are split into monthly targets, and each month contains a good mix of the simple and the complex, the important and the interesting.

## Action plan for the appraiser

There may be items where you need to take some action. It is useful to note these down, and again put dates against them
An example could be:

*By the end of April*
Inform the training manager of your support for the appraisee taking a counselling programme

# Finishing the interview

It is important to remember to finish off the appraisal interview in a way which leaves you both feeling that it has been constructive and useful. The following points give you a framework for a satisfying conclusion:

- Briefly summarize the process and reiterate your recognition of what has been achieved by the person, plus your support for their next targets.
- Refer back to what you agreed you wanted as outcomes for the interview, and check that they have been met, on both sides.
- Give the person a final opportunity to add in anything else they may want to say.
- Ensure that you give a reminder in closing that you are both real people, not just appraiser and person being appraised – a simple reference, such as 'It's lunchtime now and I realize I'm hungry' or 'Look at that, it's pouring down out there!' is enough to bring back that fundamental reality.
- Thank the individual for their preparation, participation and constructiveness, and wish them well with their targets. Remind them that if they get stuck with any of their targets, you are there to help if you can.
- Agree with the person how and when they will be given their copy of the appraisal record, and the date and time of the next appraisal, if appropriate.

# Summary

We have been looking at how we use the appraisal interview to set up the continuous improvement of the individual for the next year. It is this pattern of reviewing achievements and progress, followed by setting objectives for development over the next year, that lays the foundations for the ethos of continuous improvement. When you play your part in positively supporting and encouraging your staff, they will see this as a benefit to them, as well as to the organization.

It is important that their objectives are clearly relevant and constructive, building on what they have previously achieved. This means that they need to be job related, company related and person related. The thing to remember is that the person being appraised will know better than you do what would help them to perform even better, so your role is primarily to ensure that their action plan is achievable and realistic.

The following multiple-choice questions are a reminder of what we've covered today.

SUNDAY
MONDAY
TUESDAY
WEDNESDAY
THURSDAY
FRIDAY
SATURDAY

# Questions (answers at the back)

1. What do successful appraisals emphasize?
   a) How the person can develop even more ❏
   b) What the person needs to improve on ❏
   c) That the person achieved their goals ❏
   d) Something positive ❏

2. Why do we look for job-related development?
   a) Because that's what they're here to do – their job ❏
   b) Because they don't do their job well enough ❏
   c) To make it easier for the person to perform well in their job ❏
   d) It's what the appraisal is all about. ❏

3. Why do we look for person-related development?
   a) To find something for them to develop in ❏
   b) Because it makes them feel good ❏
   c) We don't have to – it's about their job. ❏
   d) To develop the person's potential ❏

4. What is a goal for development?
   a) Getting better at something they're not good at ❏
   b) The person performing how I want them to perform ❏
   c) Achieving a job-related task ❏
   d) The end result the person wants to achieve ❏

5. What are targets or milestones for development?
   a) The same as goals ❏
   b) Steps along the way to achieving goals ❏
   c) Things we hope they may achieve ❏
   d) The less important things ❏

6. How do we help the person being appraised to set their goals?
   a) By telling them what we've come up with for them ❏
   b) By talking about what they haven't progressed in ❏
   c) By noting down areas for potential development as we go through the first part of the interview ❏
   d) We do it for them. ❏

7. How do we help the person being appraised to sort out targets for each goal?
   a) By asking them to describe the steps they will take ❏
   b) By telling them the steps they will need to take ❏
   c) By telling them to sort them out afterwards ❏
   d) By giving them a list to choose from ❏

8. Why do we help the person being appraised to create an action plan?
   a) Because it's a section on the recording form ❏
   b) Because we want them to get some things done ❏
   c) Because that's our job ❏
   d) Because we want them to be clear about how to go about their development ❏

9. What is important about the action plan?
a) It will take a year. ❏
b) It is achievable. ❏
c) It is simple. ❏
d) It summarizes the appraisal interview. ❏

10. How do you round off the interview?
a) By signing the record of the appraisal ❏
b) By saying that you'll see them next year ❏
c) By summarizing and thanking them for their part in it ❏
d) By saying it's finished ❏

# SATURDAY

# Completing the appraisal: after the interview

When we have finished the appraisal interview, we still have a few things to do to complete the appraisal of the person. In this chapter, we will look at how you review the appraisal interview, to ensure that you continually develop your skills in conducting such interviews. Then we will give guidelines on how to follow up on actions you need to take, to make sure you fulfil your agreement with the person being appraised.

We talk about how you ensure that the right support systems are in place to help the appraisee move on their own development, including the support of other managers, other staff and possibly a mentor. Finally, we remind you that appraisals are not a one-off activity, but are part of an ongoing appraisal throughout the year, and look at how to ensure that the person's development is encouraged and supported through to their next appraisal.

# Review of appraisal

First we need to review the appraisal interview, to confirm for ourselves where it worked well and to identify how it could be improved.

This is most simply achieved by answering for ourselves some review questions. Examples would be:

- To what extent did we achieve the results/outcomes I wanted?
- What contributed to the success of the interview?
- What would have made it easier/even better?
- In what ways was the process of the interview effective?
- How else might I have made it even more effective?
- What are the key points I have learnt from this interview to help me to improve the next one?

By reviewing each appraisal interview in this way, we are practising what we are preaching to those being appraised: continuous improvement.

We are learning from the experience of conducting appraisals, so that we can fine-tune the overall guidelines to elicit the most effective results for us and for the interviewee. This continual fine-tuning is what produces excellence in conducting appraisals. It only takes a few minutes to conduct this review, and the results are well worth it.

# Actions follow-up

In the course of the appraisal interview, you may have identified certain actions which you have agreed to take. It is important to follow up on these as soon as possible after the appraisal, while they are fresh in your mind and have some priority for you. It is all too easy to be 'overtaken by events' once you have finished the interview, and to forget to take the actions.

So we need to:

- action as much as possible immediately
- record in our diaries when we will action the rest.

If nothing else, we need to make sure that the appraisal record is complete, that the person being appraised has a copy, and that our copy is properly filed.

Both the review and the actions follow-up require that you set aside an extra 15 to 30 minutes at the end of an appraisal interview, in order to complete the process.

# Support systems

So far we have dealt specifically with setting up an appraisal framework, and establishing a process for successful appraisal interviews.

However, if the approach is to be fully effective it needs to be put into the everyday work context of the individual. If we want someone to take responsibility for their own development, and to commit to targets which will enable that development, we must ensure that the relevant support systems are in place.

## 1 Other managers

In many organizations, staff may well be dealing with more than just their own line manager. It is important that others who may play a part in their development process are informed of the intention, goals and targets in that development.

These other people need to be enrolled into supporting the developments, so that the individual who has been appraised is not blocked by a lack of awareness on their part. This could be undertaken by the individual themselves, but your supporting advocacy will also be important.

Examples might be telling the training manager that you have agreed to a particular type of training programme for this individual; or asking the manager of another department to encourage this person to speak out in the working party which he/she leads.

## 2 Other staff

Sometimes the action steps we have agreed with someone will have some effect on others in the department or organization.

Again, we need to ensure that we give our direct endorsement and support in effecting any changes necessary, so that the person appraised knows that our support goes beyond fine words at the interview and into practical backing.

## 3 Organizational systems and procedures

There is no point in agreeing with someone that they can work on adapting their recording system if the overall organizational system will not allow for a deviation from the standard.

Similarly, there is no point in agreeing with someone that they can put forward a proposal for a new discussion group if there is no clear organizational procedure for doing so.

We need to ensure that organizational systems and procedures are flexible enough to accommodate any development plans the individual has.

We also need to ensure that those systems and procedures are known to the individual. Just because we know how they work, we shouldn't assume everyone else does.

## Ongoing appraisal

There is one area of continuing support which we haven't covered yet.

However motivated the person may be when they leave the appraisal interview, they now have to maintain that motivation in the midst of the pressures of everyday work and routine.

For an appraisal to be truly successful, they will need some form of 'moral support' to keep them going for their targets. It is not enough for any of us to receive a one-off boost, however positive and useful it may be. It may be six months, or even a year before the next boost, so how can we maintain the person's motivation between times? Two things can be especially effective.

## 1 We need to offer some continuing thread between one appraisal interview and the next

The way in which we do this may range from a formal arrangement through to something much more unstructured. What matters is that we demonstrate a continuing interest in and support of that individual.

Appraisal means according value, as a continuous process. People are not objects which don't usually change and can therefore be appraised just the once. People change and develop and therefore deserve continuous reassessment. What is more, the continuous reappraisal encourages and motivates them to continue to change and develop.

This may sound onerous, but you don't need to follow through by increasing the number of in-depth appraisal interviews. It is simply a matter of noticing and giving recognition to some elements of that person's development, and we can do that in a sentence in passing: 'I notice that you're enrolled on that programme – good for you!'

We also need to ensure that they know we are available to offer help if they are feeling stuck, and the offer of this help at the interview stage needs to be followed through in practice.

If someone says to you, 'I need a word with you. I'm still not getting anywhere in meetings', then you need either to give them time there and then, or to arrange a definite time to see them and talk about it. Then they will know that the offer of support and help was genuine.

Some managers may prefer to structure this support by putting in review times in between appraisals. This formalizes the opportunity to recognize progress and to offer help on areas of difficulty.

## 2 We may need to identify some form of mentor

We may, as managers, be too busy to be the reference point for all our staff in their continuing development. Rather than feel guilty because we can't offer the level of support and encouragement we would like, we can identify, with the individual concerned, someone who could fulfil that role for them.

When this is done formally, we call this person a mentor. However, it can also be set up informally. We simply identify with the individual a person whom they feel would be appropriate and useful in encouraging them to sustain their development. It may be another manager, a supervisor, a member of personnel department or a colleague.

We then talk with that person about taking on that support role with the individual.

Most people choose well when consulted, and most people are pleased to have been chosen.

# Conducting successful appraisals

We have now covered all the factors which can make a difference to the effectiveness of your appraisals.

When we go through all the different aspects of a successful appraisal, it can look like a daunting task!

So where do we start on improving our appraisals?

We can use the same principles and model for our own improvement as we do for enabling others to develop. Ask yourself, 'When I look at the full appraisal process:

● which parts do I already do well?'
● which parts do I really want to develop?'
● which parts would it be most useful to develop?'

From the answers to the second and third of these questions, establish goals and targets, and start to action them.

Remember that some of the recommendations in this guide may require some investment of time in the first place, but will save you time in the long run.

Remember that appraisals are successful when you have a clear intention in mind: to enable this individual to aim for and achieve their optimum.

Remember, above all, that you are dealing with a human being just like you. How would you like to be appraised? It's the simplest guide of all!

# Summary

In this final chapter, we have explored all the different aspects of completing the appraisal process in ways that will ensure that your appraisals successfully lead to the development of your staff.

We have emphasized the importance of ongoing support for the appraisee, so that the appraisal interview is not an isolated event. This is how you create the ethos of continuous development in the organization, so that it becomes the norm to see appraisals as a valuable part of an ongoing process of developing your people.

There is clear evidence that successful appraisal processes lead to higher retention, better morale and good overall performance. We hope that you are now able to use your appraisals to achieve these results.

The following multiple-choice questions are a reminder of what we've covered today.

SUNDAY

MONDAY

TUESDAY

WEDNESDAY

THURSDAY

FRIDAY

SATURDAY

# Questions (answers at the back)

1. Why do we review the appraisal interview?
a) Because it was a bit stilted ❏
b) Because it's the first one we've done ❏
c) To sign off that part of the task ❏
d) To check what went well and what could be improved ❏

2. How do we use our review of the appraisal?
a) To continually refine how we conduct appraisal interviews ❏
b) To revise the record of the interview ❏
c) To fill in our records of what we've done ❏
d) We don't really. ❏

3. What do we need to immediately follow up after the appraisal interview?
a) When the next one will be with this person ❏
b) Any actions we have agreed to take ❏
c) Getting the record of the interview to HR ❏
d) Other jobs we have to do ❏

4. Why do we need to take actions we have agreed?
a) We said we would. ❏
b) HR will check if we have. ❏
c) To get them off our 'To Do' list ❏
d) To show that we are genuinely supporting their ongoing development ❏

5. How can other managers support your person in their development?
a) It's my job, not theirs. ❏
b) By monitoring their actions for me ❏
c) By knowing what they want to achieve and encouraging them ❏
d) By giving them things to do ❏

6. How do we keep people motivated in their ongoing development?
a) By having some form of ongoing monitoring of their progress ❏
b) By telling them we will check how they're doing ❏
c) By picking them up on it if we notice they're not doing something they said they would ❏
d) That's up to them. ❏

7. What is important about the ongoing monitoring of their development?
a) That mistakes or failures are picked up on ❏
b) That it is positive and supportive ❏
c) That it happens in some way or other ❏
d) That the person knows they are being monitored ❏

8. What role could a mentor play?
a) Teaching the individual something they need for their development ❏
b) We don't use mentors in our organization. ❏
c) Giving the ongoing support the individual needs ❏
d) Keeping an eye on the individual ❏

9. How do we choose a mentor for someone?
a) We talk about it and ask them who would suit them. ❏
b) We identify who should do it. ❏
c) We pick someone who isn't too busy. ❏
d) We use whoever is available. ❏

10. When are appraisals finished?
a) When all the records have gone to HR ❏
b) When I've finished the interview ❏
c) When we're back to business as usual ❏
d) Never – it is a continuous process. ❏

# 7 × 7

## 1 Seven key ideas

- Link the appraisal framework to your organizational objectives, so the person will see you value their role in helping to achieve them.
- Encourage your appraisee to bring their own evidence for their achievements and progress.
- Remember that the appraisee is a human being, and take time to make them feel comfortable.
- Make sure that the appraisal is a positive process with a useful outcome for both of you.
- Treat the appraisal as an opportunity to recognize and value the appraisee's achievement.
- Emphasize the possibilities for development in the year ahead.

- Follow up on yearly appraisals with regular review of progress.

## 2 Seven best resources

- Useful guidance on performance management from an independent source which also provides useful advice on other topics: http://www.acas.org.uk/index.aspx?articleid+2927
- Useful tips on best practice: http://hrdailyadvisor.blr.com/2012/04/22/12-performance-appraisal-best-practices/#

- Clear statement of what makes the difference in effective appraisals: http://www.rave-review. net/downloads/Best%20Practices%20For%20 Successful%20Performance%20Evaluations.pdf
- *Whale Done!* by Ken Blanchard (Nicholas Brealey Publishing, 2003): A simple story of how treating staff differently can make a difference to performance.
- *It's Not Rocket Science* by Di Kamp (Metabooks, 2015): A guide to enhancing your organization through the way you treat your people.
- TED talks: leading-edge thinking on all aspects of work – http://www.ted.com/
- Your own experience of good and bad appraisals – learn from them!

# 3 Seven things to avoid

- Treating appraisals as just a tickbox to complete.
- Scheduling someone's appraisal without giving them and you time to prepare.
- Forgetting to set a positive tone to the appraisal interview.
- Rushing the appraisal interview.
- Not listening to the appraisee's views.
- Calling objectives you set 'developmental' when they are purely remedial.
- Saying: 'You're doing fine. Just keep on doing what you've been doing.'

# 4 Seven inspiring people

- Ricardo Semler, whose way of running his business inspires his staff, their customers, and innovative leaders everywhere.
- Tom Peters for always thinking of ways in which leaders can do it even better.
- Richard Branson for putting his staff and their ability first.
- Daniel Goleman for continuing to explore ways of bringing out the best in your people. See http://www.danielgoleman.info
- Nelson Mandela who demonstrated through his life that treating people well brings out the best in them.
- Herb Kelleher, founder of Southwest Airlines, who created a culture of positivity and excellent customer service by treating his staff well.
- The manager who made you feel that staff appraisals were useful, positive and valuing.

# 5 Seven great quotes

- 'Everyone likes to be recognized for a job well done, for contributions that add to a company's success. Having people feel good about the work they do is a key point, because it's through that work that we delight customers and create win-win for all.' Brian Joiner, author of *Fourth Generation Management* (McGraw-Hill, 1994)

- 'Pay special attention to those who quietly keep the place running. Often it takes a crisis for others to notice them.' Margaret Wright, author of *Mistakes Happen* (Sydney, 2006)
- 'If someone, no matter how they're trained and encouraged, is not able to perform up to standard, they shouldn't be punished. They should be in a position where they can succeed.' Ken Blanchard, author of *Whale Done!* (Nicholas Brealey Publishing, 2003)
- 'Always treat your employees exactly as you want them to treat your best customers.' Stephen R. Covey
- 'Research indicates that workers have three prime needs: interesting work, recognition for doing a good job, and being let in on things that are going on in the company.' Zig Ziglar
- 'Organizations rarely believe they're to blame when an employee underperforms. But if the company doesn't provide the opportunity for success, then people falter.' Ricardo Semler, author of *Seven-Day Weekend* (Century, 2003)
- 'The annual performance evaluation is your most valuable motivational tool. The only downside is that it might require you to talk to your employees more than once a year. But don't worry: you can usually count on moving to a new assignment before that's necessary.' Scott Adams, author of *Dogbert's Management Handbook* (HarperCollins Publishers, 1998)

## 6 Seven things to do today

- Start the process of linking appraisal objectives in your area to the overall business objectives.
- Diary in some one-to-ones with your team members, and use them to ask them how they are doing with their objectives.
- Check that you have taken all the actions you promised at the last round of appraisals, and if not, apologize and do it!
- Make a note to file with previous appraisals when someone does something well.
- Notice *how* people do their work/work with colleagues, not just *what* they do.
- Make a list for yourself of possible developmental objectives for staff in your area.
- Start collecting evidence for your own next appraisal.

## 7 Seven trends for tomorrow

- More acknowledgement of the need to link individual appraisal objectives to the overall business objectives.
- More emphasis on behavioural objectives in conjunction with practical objectives – blending the what and the how.
- Appraisals becoming more of a summary of the reviews of the previous twelve months.

- People may be called 'human resources', but we need to treat them as valuable human beings – they are essential to the success of your organization – and they will leave if they don't feel recognized for the part they play.
- People are busier than ever. Make sure you leave enough time to prepare for and implement appraisals properly.
- Research suggests that young talent wants more from a job than just money – they expect to have opportunities for development.
- An emphasis on generic core skills as people change career more often in the course of their work lives.

# Answers

**Sunday:** 1a, b, c; 2b, c, d;
3a, c, d; 4b, c, d; 5a, b, c;
6a, b, d; 7a, b, c; 8b, c, d;
9a, c, d; 10a, b, d

**Monday:** 1b, c, d; 2a, c, d;
3a, b, d; 4a, c, d; 5a, b, c;
6b, c, d; 7a, c, d; 8a, b, d;
9b, c, d; 10a, c, d

**Tuesday:** 1b, c, d; 2a, b, d;
3a, c, d; 4b, c, d; 5a, b, c;
6a, c, d; 7a, b, d; 8b, c, d;
9a, b, d; 10a, c, d

**Wednesday:** 1a, b, d; 2a, c, d;
3a, b, c; 4a, b, c; 5b, c, d;
6a, c, d; 7a, b, d; 8b, c, d;
9a, b, c; 10a, c, d

**Thursday:** 1b, c, d; 2a, b, d;
3a, c, d; 4a, c, d; 5a, b, c;
6a, b, d; 7b, c, d; 8 a, c, d;
9a, b, c; 10a, b, d

**Friday:** 1b, c, d; 2a, b, d;
3a, b, c; 4a, b, c; 5a, c, d;
6a, b, d; 7b, c, d; 8a, b, c;
9a, c, d; 10a, b, d

**Saturday:** 1a, b, c; 2b, c, d;
3a, c, d; 4a, b, c; 5a, b, d;
6b, c, d; 7a, c, d; 8a, b, d;
9b, c, d; 10a, b, d

# Notes

# ALSO AVAILABLE IN THE 'IN A WEEK' SERIES

APPRAISALS • BRAND MANAGEMENT • BUSINESS PLANS • CONTENT MARKETING • COVER LETTERS • DIGITAL MARKETING • DIRECT MARKETING • EMOTIONAL INTELLIGENCE • FINDING & HIRING TALENT • JOB HUNTING • LEADING TEAMS • MARKET RESEARCH • MARKETING • MBA • MOBILE MARKETING • NETWORKING • OUTSTANDING CONFIDENCE • PEOPLE MANAGEMENT • PLANNING YOUR CAREER • PROJECT MANAGEMENT • SMALL BUSINESS MARKETING • STARTING A NEW JOB • TACKLING TOUGH INTERVIEW QUESTIONS • TIME MANAGEMENT

For information about other titles in the 'In A Week' series, please visit
www.teachyourself.co.uk

# MORE TITLES AVAILABLE IN THE 'IN A WEEK' SERIES

ADVANCED NEGOTIATION SKILLS • ASSERTIVENESS • BUSINESS ECONOMICS • COACHING • COPYWRITING • DECISION MAKING • DIFFICULT CONVERSATIONS • ECOMMERCE • FINANCE FOR NON-FINANCIAL MANAGERS • JOB INTERVIEWS • MANAGING STRESS AT WORK • MANAGING YOUR BOSS • MANAGING YOURSELF • MINDFULNESS AT WORK • NEGOTIATION SKILLS • NLP • PEOPLE SKILLS • PSYCHOMETRIC TESTING • SEO AND SEARCH MARKETING • SOCIAL MEDIA MARKETING • START YOUR OWN BUSINESS • STRATEGY • SUCCESSFUL SELLING • UNDERSTANDING AND INTERPRETING ACCOUNTS

For information about other titles in the 'In A Week' series, please visit www.teachyourself.co.uk